THE
CHEAP
BOOK

HOW BOOKS

Cincinnati, Ohio
www.howdesign.com

THE
CHEAP
BOOK

the official guide to embracing your inner cheapskate

Robin Herbst & Julie Miller
with illustrations by Mike Farley

THE CHEAP BOOK. Copyright © 2008 by Robin Herbst and Julie Miller. Printed in Canada.
All rights reserved. No other part of this book may be reproduced in any form or by any electronic or
mechanical means including information storage and retrieval systems without permission in writing from the publisher, except by a reviewer, who may quote brief passages in a review. Published
by HOW Books, an imprint of F+W Publications, Inc., 4700 East Galbraith Road, Cincinnati, Ohio
45236. (800) 289-0963. First edition.

For more fine books from F+W Publications, visit www.fwpublications.com.

12 11 10 09 08   5 4 3 2 1

Distributed in Canada by Fraser Direct, 100 Armstrong Avenue, Georgetown, Ontario, Canada L7G
5S4, Tel: (905) 877-4411. Distributed in the U.K. and Europe by David & Charles, Brunel House,
Newton Abbot, Devon, TQ12 4PU, England, Tel: (+44) 1626-323200, Fax: (+44) 1626-323319, E-mail:
postmaster@davidandcharles.co.uk. Distributed in Australia by Capricorn Link, P.O. Box 704,
Windsor, NSW 2756 Australia, Tel: (02) 4577-3555.

Library of Congress Cataloging-in-Publication Data

Herbst, Robin and Miller, Julie.
 The cheap book : the official guide to embracing your inner cheapskate / Robin Herbst and Julie
Miller ; with illustrations by Mike Farley. -- 1st ed.
     p. cm.
 Includes index.
 ISBN-13: 978-1-60061-097-4 (pbk. : alk. paper)
 1. Consumer education. 2. Home economics--Accounting. 3. Finance, Personal. 4. Finance,
Personal--Humor. I. Miller, Julie. II. Title.
 TX335.H4675 2008
 332.024--dc22   2007047839

Edited by Michelle Ehrhard, Amy Schell
Designed by Grace Ring
Illustrations by Mike Farley
Production coordinated by Greg Nock

F+W PUBLICATIONS, INC.

ABOUT THE AUTHORS

Robin and Julie have been friends for more than twenty-eight years, sharing cheap tendencies and encouraging each other's cheap ways. They both grew up in Edina, Minnesota.

Robin is a CPA, and has been working as a tax accountant for nineteen years. She lives with her husband in Inver Grove Heights, Minnesota. When not collaborating with Julie on cheapisms, she enjoys family, friends and her menagerie of cats and fish.

Julie is a director at a Fortune 100 company and lives with her husband, three dogs and her cat in Bloomington, Minnesota. When not collaborating with Robin on cheapisms, she enjoys golf, shopping for shoes and purses, and is an avid gardener.

Please visit our web site at www.thecheapbook.com for more laughs and silly gift ideas.

ACKNOWLEDGMENTS

We would like to dedicate this book to our husbands and the many friends and family who have inspired us and contributed their cheapisms and stories. Their cheap antics remind us of how important it is to laugh at our ridiculous frugalities.

We would like to thank Courtney Lewis Opdahl and Dana Mack for their help in editing our material.

A special thanks to Mike Farley for all of his wonderful ideas and illustrations.

This book is a celebration of true friendship and fun relationships.

TABLE OF CONTENTS

INTRODUCTION

ARE YOU ONE OF US?

Do you recycle greeting cards and holiday wrap? Have you saved tinfoil
so you can reuse it later? Are you a re-gifter? If you answered yes to any of
these questions, you are One of Us!

Julie   Robin

We never wanted to be cheap. Cheapness is not a trait one is born with, encoded in one's DNA. Cheapness is an art form, one we've acquired over time and finally shared with one another—an attribute we concealed throughout many years of friendship. There was relief in our admission to each other (whew!) and to our families, who could finally put to rest the notion that our quirks were some form of penny-pinching disorder. Perhaps others are unable to classify us as cheap because the term calls to mind grand, cash-crunching gestures. We're not talking dine-and-ditch or bad tips at classy restaurants kind of cheapness. We're talking shoddy, chintzy, too-embarrassed-to-admit-our-tight-fisted-ways kind of cheap.

This book celebrates our frugal oddities. We hope that you, too, will be able to admit to your stingy ways and join us proudly in our crusade for never-ending penny-pinching!

DEFINING CHEAP

If we allow a traditional definition to pigeonhole cheapness, the insults would defeat us. *Webster's Dictionary* defines *cheap* as "deserving of scorn, contemptible" and labels a cheap item as something "of little value or poor quality; virtually worthless." But *cheap* is also noted as "spending or able to spend little" and "costing little labor or trouble," which supports our rationale: Taking the cheap road is the wisest path. Able to spend little? Clearly the Cheapo is clever. Costing little labor or trouble? Obviously the Cheapo suffers less stress. Since the dawn of the cheapest man and woman, these misers have been misunderstood due to unsatisfactory definitions. We say *cheap* is a means of saving money by the innovative use or non-use of materials and talents without regard to societal norms. A Cheapo could be called a rebel. Time and time again, history's nonconformists have been trendsetters. Correcting the poor perception of cheapness is the first step; therefore, just as Michael Jackson's *Bad* was good, cheap is smart.

CHEAP FACTOR SCORING

Throughout the book, you'll notice an ongoing score for each *cheapism* (defined in our Cheapo Glossary as "the act of saving money by the innovative use or non-use of materials and talents without regard to societal norms"). As you read and discover your cheapness on each page, tally your score on the sheet provided at the end of the book. This process will give you a gauge to measure the depth of your cheapness, and separate the sensible from the shoddy. You may be surprised at your rank.

 Cheap Factor 1 = Sensible

 Cheap Factor 2 = Thrifty

 Cheap Factor 3 = Frugal

Cheap Factor 4 = Stingy

 Cheap Factor 5 = Cheap

 Cheap Factor 10 = Beyond tacky, perhaps disgusting, borderline insane. There is no word in the English language to describe this level of cheapness. Anyone who admits to being this cheap should submit his or her name and story for consideration in the Cheapo Hall of Fame at www.thecheapbook.com.

To get you started, here's a little warm-up quiz.

- Do you only buy used textbooks at college? You score a 1.
- Does your family vacation consist of sleeping in a tent and fishing and hiking for fun? You score a 2.
- When the bar of soap in the bathroom becomes so small you can't hold onto it, do you meld it with a new bar of soap? You score a 3.
- Do you tear your fabric softener sheets in half when drying clothes? You score a 4.
- Would you use a coupon on your first date and make her pay half the bill? You score a 5.
- Do you save your calendars so you can reuse them ten years later? You score a 10.

CHAPTER 1

CHEAPNESS
STARTS AT HOME

overflowing bags

special draw string bag →

supper

"secret" stash

cheap 2 factor

No. 1

You save all plastic bags for reuse. Throwing out an empty plastic bag is a punishable offense.

No. 2

Duct tape is your preferred bonding agent. It can be used to mend broken windows, hang posters, fix plumbing and repair old shoes. It's a thing of beauty!

cheap factor 2

SEE ALSO **MANTAPE** IN THE CHEAPO GLOSSARY, PAGE 207.

mend broken windows

(use with clear garbage bags for full effect.)

very sticky

roll inside-out as poster hanger

A thing of beauty.

repair old shoes

fix plumbing

No. 3

You resort to using a fingernail file or other tool to get the last remnant of lip balm when it won't push up any farther.

cheap **1** factor

SEE ALSO **CHAPSTICKS** IN CHEAPO INVENTIONS, PAGE 174.

No. 4
You spend time monitoring the electric meter,
taking measures to slow down the rotations.

No. 5
Leaving lights on has become public enemy number one. You're constantly telling your family to flip the switch.

No. 6
Any sunflower seeds that have not been cracked open are returned to the bird feeder.

No. 7
You don't use holiday lights
because they use too much electricity.

No. 8
You spread your yard fertilizer on thin to put off buying additional bags.

No. 9
You painstakingly arrange the sprinkler
so it perfectly covers the lawn, yet
does not hit the pavement.

No. 10
In the colder months, you set the thermostat
low believing that body heat and
layering will make up the difference.

How low can you go?

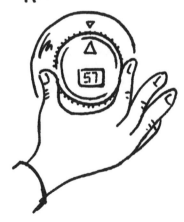

No. 11

Break the seal on a new bottle of water
each time you run dry? No way! That bottle can
be refilled over and over (and over).

$1 FOR ALL 3!

stress toy

Bifocals

DOLLAR MART

Shoe horn

No. 12

You regularly shop at the dollar store
and know which location has the best deals.

cheap 1 factor

No. 14
You've taken all the time it requires to understand the rules of your long-distance service.

cheap factor 3

Looky here... extra charges after 7pm on Tuesdays.

No. 15
You stop using regular trash bags
in favor of grocery store plastic bags.
You'll never have to buy a trash bag again!

cheap **2** factor

Is there a choice?

vs.

Walmart

Walmart

glee

Free ☐

26¢ ☐

No. 16

You keep a pair of scissors near the paper towels
to cut even the "select-a-size" towels in half.

CHAPTER 2

BATHROOM
CHEAPISMS

No. 17

You use a tissue over and over
until it literally falls apart.

SEE ALSO **KLEENO** IN CHEAPO
INVENTIONS, PAGE 177.

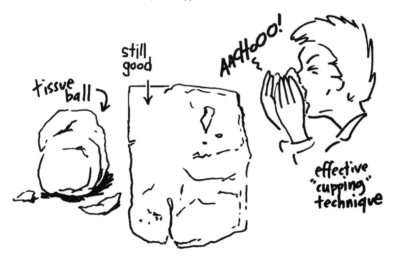

cheap factor

4

No. 18

You use medication years beyond its expiration date.

No. 19

You have fourteen-day disposable contacts, and you still wear them on day twenty-four. (Score yourself a 5 if you still wear them with a piece missing.)

cheap **4** factor

contact vision-test

No. 20
You save cotton out of vitamin or medicine bottles and use it for other purposes.

from wadding to
nail polish remover.

No. 21
You use baking soda instead of toothpaste.

cheap
2
factor

No. 22

Your guests probably won't notice
if you hide your fancy lotions
and pull out the generic brands.
(This works for a whole host of
bathroom products, including dental
floss, hair gel and shaving cream.)

cheap 3 factor

No. 23

After showering, you use expensive fragrant lotions on your upper body and inexpensive lotion on your legs and feet. (After all, you can't really smell your legs.)

No. 24
You painstakingly peel the last shreds of toilet paper off the cardboard roll.

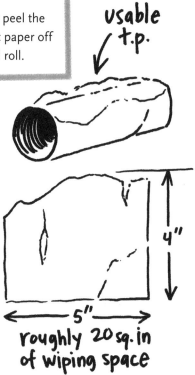

usable t.p.

4"

← 5" →

roughly 20 sq. in
of wiping space

No. 25
You meld soap bits together
to make a bigger, more usable bar.

tremendous
pressure

exerted in
shower to
combine
soap bits.

bending
over
adds
extra
pressure

No. 26
Your family credo is: "If it's yellow,
let it mellow. If it's brown, flush it down."

No. 27

You count the squares of toilet paper,
using only the amount needed for the job.

SEE ALSO **CROFINGER** IN THE CHEAPO GLOSSARY, PAGE 205.

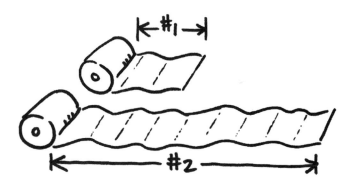

No. 29
Toilet paper multitasking: You blow your
nose, and then use the toilet paper to wipe.

No. 30
They say you should replace your razor once a week…hogwash! You replace yours only after it draws blood or starts pulling the hairs out.

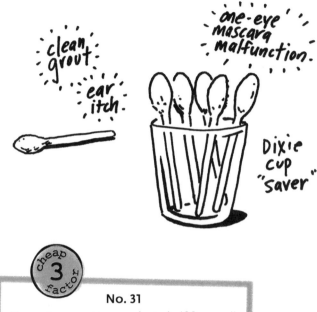

No. 31

You cut your cotton swabs in half for small jobs and save the other half for later.

No. 32

You take all measures and strength to get the last remnant out of a tube of toothpaste.

SEE ALSO **EXTRACTOTENACITY** IN THE CHEAPO GLOSSARY, PAGE 205.

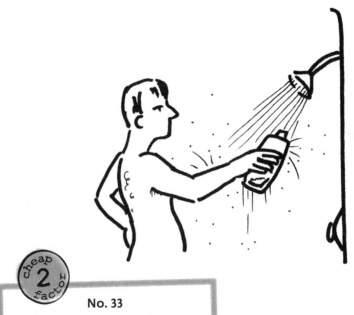

No. 33
You mix water with your shampoo
to make it last longer.

No. 34

Rather than spend money on a hair care
professional, you have your partner cut your hair.
Ladies, watch out for the electric shaver.

No. 35
You actually have tried pasting together
the unused portion of white strips
to get another seven days of whitening.
(If only it were that easy.)

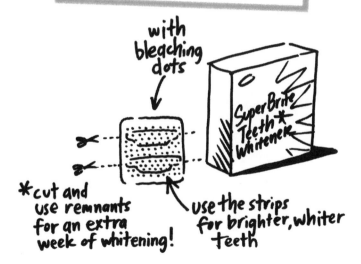

with
bleaching
dots

SuperBrite
Teeth *
Whitener

*cut and
use remnants
for an extra
week of whitening!

use the strips
for brighter, whiter
teeth

No. 36
After spilling shampoo or shower gel,
you try to scoop it up quickly
before it washes down the drain.

cheap
3
factor

SEE ALSO **SWOOP 'N' SCOOP**
IN THE CHEAPO GLOSSARY,
PAGE 208.

Swoop-n-scoop
away from
drain.

CHAPTER 2

CHAPTER 3

KITCHEN
CHEAP

No. 37
You keep the oven door open after
cooking in winter to reduce heating costs.

No. 38
You erase the pencil markings
on paper so you can reuse it.

"Make sure you save the plastic wear."

STUNT MAN

cheap **2** factor

No. 39

You wash plastic plates and utensils
so you can reuse them.
(Cheapo Bonus Tip: Most plastic utensils
can be washed in the dishwasher.)

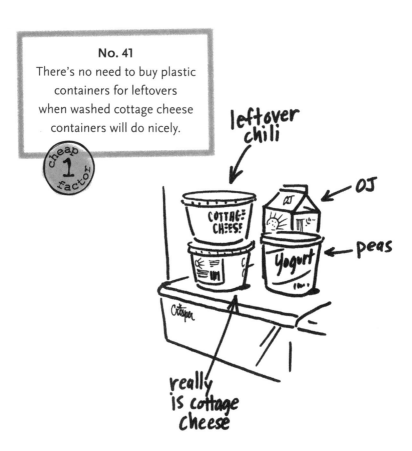

No. 41
There's no need to buy plastic containers for leftovers when washed cottage cheese containers will do nicely.

cheap factor 1

leftover chili

OJ

peas

COTTAGE CHEESE

Yogurt

Crisper

really is cottage cheese

No. 42
You wash out and reuse
your resealable plastic bags.

SEE ALSO **FAILED ATTEMPTS AT CHEAPNESS,** PAGE 181.

Zippy Seal

Dry foods

Empty + Re-use

Meats + messy foods

only then to trash.

No. 43
You save tinfoil to reuse later.

SEE ALSO **THE ALUMINIZER** IN
CHEAPO INVENTIONS, PAGE 178.

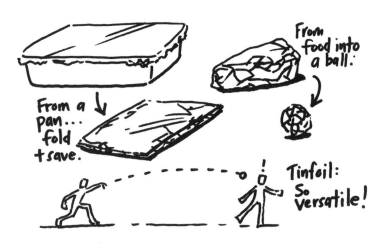

From a pan... fold + save.

From food into a ball.

Tinfoil: So versatile!

CHAPTER 4

CHEAP IDEAS
FOR PETS

No. 44

Skip having pets.

No. 45
Your child's discarded stuffed
animals make great dog toys.
(Warning: Make sure you've obtained
your child's permission first.)

Find a bag with handles and its a spinning toy!

No. 46
Grocery bags make for all-purpose cat toys.

No. 47

You teach your cat how to use the toilet.

(Tip: Don't teach her how to flush.)

Nobody said it would be easy.

cheap factor 1

No. 48
You reuse plastic bags from prior
purchases for cat scoopings or dog doo.
(Warning: Always check for holes!)

SEE ALSO **POOSMUDGE** IN THE CHEAPO GLOSSARY, PAGE 207.

CHEAP IDEAS
FOR KIDS

No. 50
Skip having children.

No. 51
You cut the fingertips off
unraveled dollar store gloves to make
cool action wear for your kids.

mama...

No. 52
Extend the use of diapers—they can
hold up to ten pounds of liquid!

cheap factor

cheap factor 2

No. 53
Your younger children have
only worn cutoffs for shorts.

No. 54
You've convinced your kids to eagerly
await the church rummage sale
to get their "new" toys and clothes.

cheap
3
factor

---

cheap
3
factor

No. 55

You stockpile Halloween costumes
for years to come. (Note: If your children
don't want to dress up in last year's
costume, give them an old sheet and
a pair of scissors.)

No. 56
You buy your toddler a dog toy
because it costs less than a child's toy.

GLO BRITE

VS.

Mr. Soapy Big Bubbles

$0.99

$3.79

cheap factor 3

No. 57
You use dishwashing liquid
for your kid's bubble bath.

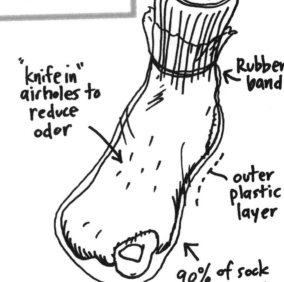

No. 58
You make your children wear plastic bags over their socks when their shoes or boots have holes in them.

"knife in" airholes to reduce odor

Rubber band

outer plastic layer

90% of sock is still good.

CHAPTER 6

CLEANING
CHEAPISMS

No. 59

You reuse your fabric softener sheets
multiple times or cut them in half.
(You're convinced that clothes are just as
soft after two uses of one dryer sheet.)

Use scissors,
tearing uses
too much
scent.

No. 60
You discontinue your garbage
service and use the neighbor's can
(only under the cover of night).

No. 61
You use an old nylon stocking as
a lint trap on your washing machine hose.

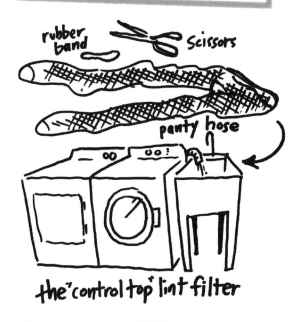

rubber band

Scissors

panty hose

the "control top" lint filter

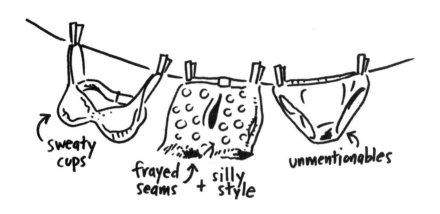

sweaty cups

frayed ↑ silly
seams + style

unmentionables

cheap 2 factor

No. 62

You hang your clothes out to dry—including veteran
undergarments—instead of running the dryer.

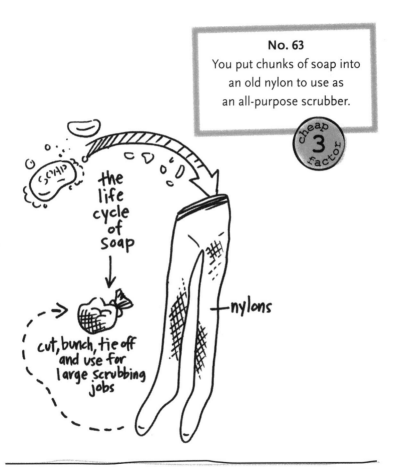

No. 63
You put chunks of soap into an old nylon to use as an all-purpose scrubber.

cheap **3** factor

the life cycle of soap

SOAP

cut, bunch, tie off and use for large scrubbing jobs

nylons

No. 64

Your sponges go through the cycle of life. First, you use a new sponge in the kitchen; once stinky it gets demoted to the bathroom; and finally it gets sent on a life-ending mission such as cleaning the grill or the cat box.

cheap 4 factor

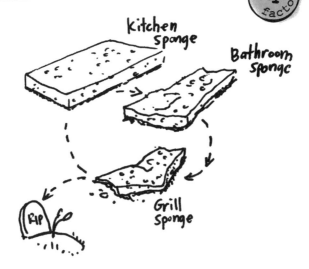

Kitchen Sponge

Bathroom Sponge

Grill Sponge

RIP

CHEAPLY
GARBED

No. 65

You continue to wear a watch
after the battery has died—even a broken
watch is still right twice a day.

It doesn't run,
but it looks
good!

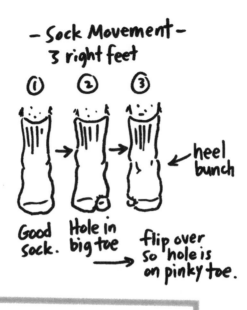

- Sock Movement -
3 right feet

① ② ③

→ → ← heel bunch

Good sock. | Hole in big toe → | flip over so hole is on pinky toe.

cheap 4 factor

No. 66

You move a sock to the other foot to
continue using it. Rotating it so the hole is not
visible can also extend your sock's life.
This can be done with nylon stockings as well.

No. 67

Nail polish is a mainstay if you are a nylon
wearer. Only after three strikes is the nylon out:
run in toe, run in thigh, and loose waist elastic.

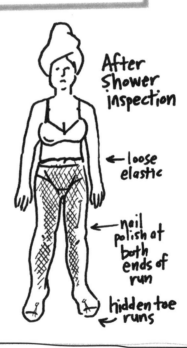

After
Shower
inspection

← loose
elastic

← nail
polish at
both
ends of
run

← hidden toe
runs

the key is the buckle.

cheap factor 1

No. 68

Reversible belts are required in a Cheapo's wardrobe.

No. 69
You use safety pins to hold your bra straps together.
Actually, this isn't cheap—it's just sad.

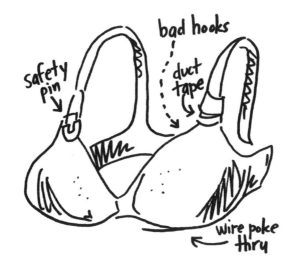

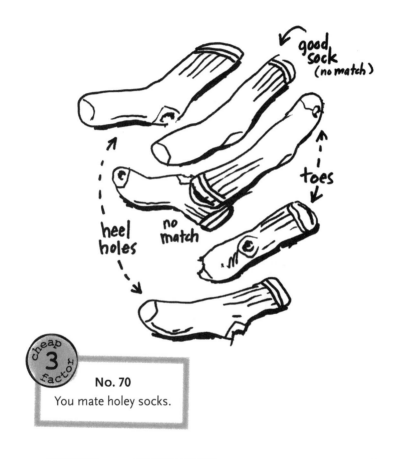

good
sock
(no match)

toes

heel
holes

no
match

cheap
3
factor

No. 70

You mate holey socks.

No. 71
You don't replace your underwear
until it becomes well-ventilated.

SEE ALSO **SUPERWEAR** IN THE
CHEAPO GLOSSARY, PAGE 207.

CHAPTER 7

"genuine" diamonique

vs.

No. 72
You boast that you're wearing knock-off perfume or jewelry.

cheap **4** factor

you know it's bad when you've used up the color you hate.

lost & mangled bristles

No. 73
Your makeup mantra is: "Use it till it's dried up or gone." Experts say makeup should be tossed after six months. Hogwash!

No. 74

You don't buy clothes labeled "dry clean only," because there's no way you're going to pay someone else to do your laundry.

No. 75

You purchase clothes that are the wrong size because the price is right. (Clothing that is too tight or too loose is fashionable anyway...right?)

No. 76
You buy a fancy dress for a special occasion and leave the tag on so you can return it the next day—careful not to spill or get those pesky white deodorant stains!

ENTERTAINING THE
CHEAP WAY

No. 77
If your friends left something behind
at your last party, you deny it.

No. 78

You use 3.5 oz. paper cups for your guests.

90

No. 79

You ask your guests in advance how many cups of coffee they will be drinking so you can brew the right amount. Why make more if you don't need to?

Dinner Party Coffee List:

Ted - 2
Alice - 1
Jean - 3
Bill - no/tea
Carol - 1
Mark - 1
Joe - 2
Me - 2

⑫

No. 80
You don't have cable TV or a satellite dish,
and you're still using rabbit ears.

No. 81
You reuse paper plates
that only have minimal stains.

toast? Maybe.

Corn on the cob?
No.

No. 82
You refill your premium liquor bottles
with cheap booze for parties.

No. 83

You bring out the dollar store brand toilet paper, paper towels and tissues before your guests arrive.

cheap factor 4

VS.

THIN & CRISPY

Daisy Soft

No. 84

When giving guests leftovers from a meal, you put the edibles in bags with twist ties rather than plastic containers or resealable bags.

cheap **3** factor

"Ready in a sec..."

Ahh, dandelions. So very chic!

cheap factor 4

No. 85
Under the guise of being chic,
you serve your guests a dandelion salad.

GIFTING
CHEAPLY

No. 87

You're a re-gifter. (Tip: Be sure to remove any evidence that it was originally a gift to you.)

SEE ALSO **FAILED ATTEMPTS AT CHEAPNESS**, PAGE 185.

It's yours!   It's theirs!   It's yours again!

Fold used wrap neatly into handled bags for even more savings.

No. 88

You reuse gift wrap.

cheap **4** factor

No. 89
You regularly shop garage sales
and clearance racks for gifts.
(Tip: Use extra care to remove the
entire colored clearance tag.)

No. 90

You actually give a large empty box
to a child as a present. It makes a great fort.

Who knew that plastic could be so pretty?

No. 92
You use plastic bags to make
woven rugs for fun and profit.
Plus, people love homemade gifts!

CHAPTER 10

AUTOMOTIVE
CHEAP

No. 93

You speak reverently of the low gas prices
your father remembered.

> **No. 94**
> You never stomp on the gas pedal
> because the sudden acceleration wastes fuel.

No. 95

You use dish detergent to wash your car.

No. 97
You use your windshield wiper fluid sparingly,
even if it compromises visibility.

cheap **3** factor

No. 98

Or—you jockey behind another car whose driver is using his windshield wiper fluid, so you don't have to use your own. (Hint: This works best at freeway speeds.)

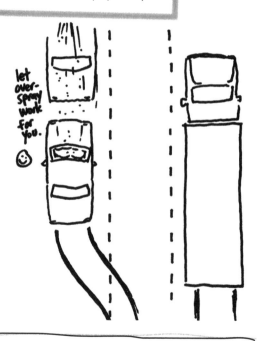

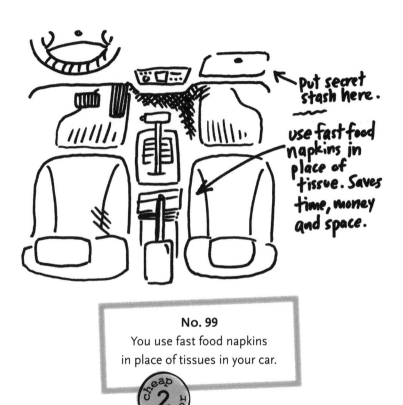

put secret stash here.

use fast food napkins in place of tissue. Saves time, money and space.

No. 99
You use fast food napkins
in place of tissues in your car.

cheap 2 factor

No. 100
You still look sharp by keeping one side of your car in mint condition, while you jury-rig the opposite side.
(After all, you can only see one side at a time.)

cheap factor 3

Duct taped, dented door + hubcapless wheels on opposite side.

Nice ride, Steve.

CHAPTER 11

DINING
CHEAP

No. 101
When eating out, you check the entrée prices
first and order based on cost, not desire.

No. 102
You purchase one small soda and ask
for extra cups for the rest of your family...
filling up their cups from your "bottomless"
cup somehow doesn't seem wrong.

No. 103
You mix dry concentrate milk with water
to stretch the number of servings from your milk
carton. (It still tastes the same, doesn't it?)

Add 2:1 skim to dry mix
Serve very cold.

mmmm...

Instant
Milk

*In your world...
it's you vs. them.*

No. 104
You eat leftovers that are borderline rancid—
especially chicken, fish, pork and eggs.

Looks like there's enough for one last cup.

cheap 3 factor

No. 105
You reuse your tea bags.
(Score yourself a 4 if you reuse
the tea bag more than twice.)

cheap 3 factor

No. 106

With a little scraping and enough cinnamon, even burnt toast is edible.

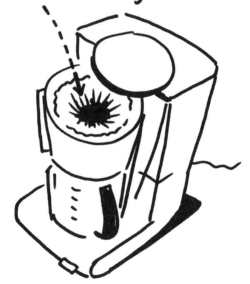

No. 108
You re-warm your coffee rather than make a fresh cup. (Score yourself a 4 if you've re-warmed the next day.)

Reheated coffee is like stepping back into the old West. for a cup of ol' Joe.

No. 109
You cut the mold off of the cheese block and continue to use. (Score yourself a 4 if you do this with bread.)

↑
moldy
end

moldy
end

Slice of cheese + half of sub bread still make a great sandwich.

No. 110

Fresh from the bakery, you can eat a slice of bread by itself. The loaf moves to sandwich use next, then toast, and then croutons. An elderly loaf is used for bread crumbs, but the true end of its life cycle is when the birds get it.

cheap
4
factor

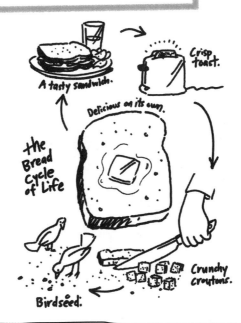

A tasty sandwich.

Crisp toast.

Delicious on its own.

the Bread Cycle of Life

Crunchy croutons.

Birdseed.

No. 111

You alter the expiration date on items in order
to trick family members into using them longer.
(An extra fine permanent marker and a steady
hand help pull this one off.)

A good marker
can turn
any number
into an 8!

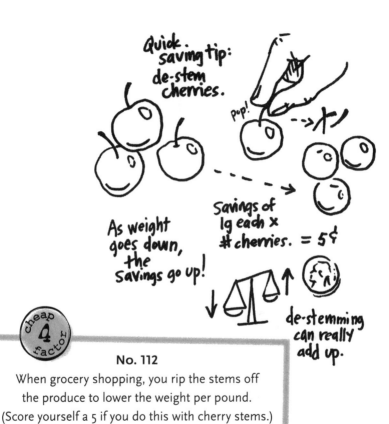

Quick saving tip: de-stem cherries.

pop!

As weight goes down, the savings go up!

Savings of 1g each x # cherries. = 5¢

de-stemming can really add up.

cheap factor 4

No. 112

When grocery shopping, you rip the stems off
the produce to lower the weight per pound.
(Score yourself a 5 if you do this with cherry stems.)

No. 113

You buy next year's holiday candy in January. (Note: Chocolate becomes white around the edges after a while, but it is still edible.)

"Save some of those."

No. 114
You save unused paper napkins
from restaurants to use at home.

No. 115
You bring the uneaten rolls from
a restaurant home to use instead of birdseed.

so what
if it has
spaghetti
sauce on it...

No. 116

When going out to dinner, you won't order the side salad because it's not included with the meal.

cheap 5 factor

No. 117
You take your family to the grocery store's free sample day for dinner. Who knew that eating baked beans, crab cakes and pickles out of paper cups could be so filling?

No. 118
You save your chewed gum for later,
making it part of the dining experience.

cheap
3
factor

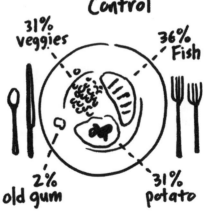

The New
Dinner Portion
Control

31%
veggies

36%
Fish

2%
old gum

31%
potato

No. 119

You save the soy sauce packets from Chinese takeout and empty them into your own decanter. Fortune cookie says, "Be loud, be proud, be cheap!"

cheap **4** factor

oooh, save those.

No. 120

You save salt, pepper, sugar and utensil packets from airplane meals. This tip is perhaps a little outdated since the airlines are becoming Cheapos themselves!

No. 121
You buy food that you don't like
just because you have a coupon for it.

CHAPTER 11

No. 122

You pretend that you're getting a child his lunch by ordering the kids meal at the drive-through, but you eat it yourself.

"Don't worry, I'll bring back your casserole pan..."

No. 123
You unabashedly take home the leftovers
if your host mentions throwing anything out.
(Be sure to return all pans and utensils promptly.)

cheap factor 1

OFFICE
CHEAP

No. 124

You don't write on calendars
so you can reuse them ten years later.

No. 125

Tissue multitasking: You use a tissue to blow your nose and wipe off your computer monitor. (Hint: The mistake to avoid is blowing your nose first without allowing the tissue to dry before wiping the screen.)

No. 126
They think you're the office hero
for bringing in treats, when really you brought
made-at-home rejects or oldies.

No. 127

You use the right size sticky note for the job.
(You keep all sizes handy and do a little analysis
to determine which size fits best.)

cheap
2
factor

No. 128

You extend your office stash by confiscating staples, notepads and paper clips from two cubicles away. (Warning: This is best done after-hours, but can be considered appropriate compensation for unpaid overtime.)

cheap 3 factor

No. 129

You pick up flavored coffee creamer and sturdy plastic utensils from the company cafeteria.

cheap
3
factor

No. 130
Bagels, donuts, chips and leftover
luncheon meats make great freebie meals.
(Warning: Do not pilfer from the community
fridge! Some items have been in there
longer than you've been with the company.)

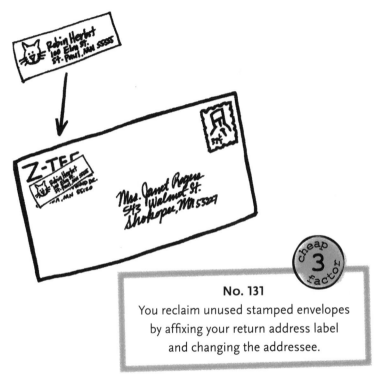

No. 131
You reclaim unused stamped envelopes
by affixing your return address label
and changing the addressee.

SEE ALSO **CHEAP STORIES**, PAGE 197.

No. 132
You immediately cover markers after use
to prevent them from drying out too quickly.

CHEAP
DATES

No. 133

Don't tell your date that you've merely re-warmed
your leftovers for her "home-cooked meal."
(Throw some parsley and a fresh strawberry on
the side, and she'll never know.)

No. 134
You use coupons on your first date.
(Score yourself a 5 if you still make your
date pay half the bill.)

No. 136
Under the guise of romance, you take
your date on a picnic rather than to one
of those expensive restaurants.

cheap
2
factor

No. 138

When taking your date to a movie, you sneak your own snacks into the theatre. (Score yourself a 3 if you sneak in soda. Score yourself a 4 if you sneak in alcohol, and a 5 if you bring your own coffee.)

The Theatre Handbag

soda

popcorn

gum

licorice

No. 139
You're not too ashamed to treat
your date to discounted movies.

CHEAP
VACATIONS

No. 141
You convince your spouse that camping really is fun: a free place to sleep, you bring your own food and enjoy all that cheap, fresh air!

No. 142

Your main activities on vacation are hiking and fishing. Boy, are those easy on the pocketbook (and everyone loves fishing)!

No. 143

You pack loaves of bread, peanut butter and jelly for the car instead of stopping at those overpriced fast-food restaurants.

No. 144

Rather than wipe the excess sunscreen on a towel (or even worse, on a paper product that you'll just throw away), you find someone nearby who will accept the sunscreen, and make the transfer. This works great with lotion too!

cheap factor 4

CHAPTER 15

CHEAPISMS
FOR STUDENTS

No. 145
Get your hair cut as short as possible to prolong
time between visits to the discount salon.

No. 146
You take advantage of every nearby gym's
free trial offer, one after another,
so you don't actually have to join.

oh yeah,
Damien's good
for the rent.

cheap 1 factor

No. 148

You only buy used textbooks. You don't even
need to read them because the prior owner has
already highlighted the important stuff for you!

No. 149
You open up bank accounts to get the free gifts.

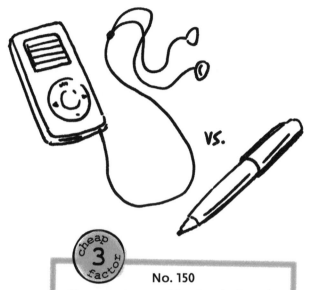

VS.

No. 150
You attend career fairs that don't apply
to your major because they offer better
free stuff at the vendor booths.

No. 151
Ramen noodles and mac 'n' cheese
are two of your five basic food groups.

CHEAPO
INVENTIONS

THE TOOL: 1001 USES!

A "handcrafted" wire hanger does the job of a hundred tools. Its functions include, but are not limited to: drain de-clogging, bird feeder cleaning, belt pulling, TV reception fixing, mouse trap removing, and hundreds more!

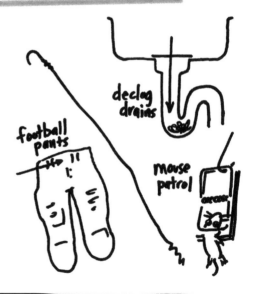

declog drains

football pants

mouse patrol

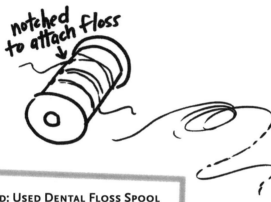

notched to attach floss ↓

THE SPOLD: USED DENTAL FLOSS SPOOL
For those Cheapos who reuse their
dental floss, the Spold also holds strings
and works best for small jobs.

CHAPSTICKS: ANCIENT CHINESE SECRET
Why waste the last of the lip balm?
Scooping it out stretches the wax for weeks.

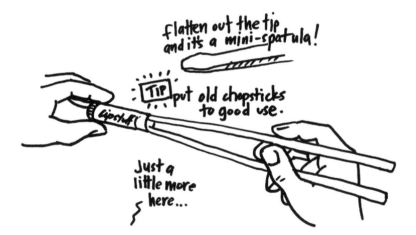

flatten out the tip and it's a mini-spatula!

TIP put old chopsticks to good use.

Just a little more here...

THE CATLITE 3000: EXERCISE CATS WITH LIGHT!
Cats love to strike at the beam on the
wall or floor. It's fun for the whole family,
while Tigger gets a good workout.

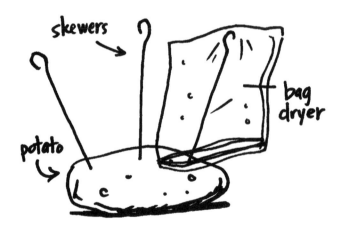

pencil made
airholes
(ventilated)

wire
attachment
for faster
drying

Kleenō

*USE
AT YOUR
OWN RISK

**KLEENO: THE SECRET STORAGE BOX
OF USED TISSUES**

This recycled tissue box with hang-drying
attachment is perfect for those who
reuse their tissues. Half-used tissues need
a home (and a hiding spot)!

Nifty
Accordion
Tinfoil Organizer

aluminum foil

Balled tin
does not work.

FAILED ATTEMPTS AT CHEAPNESS

> Reheating un-popped popcorn
> kernels to squeeze out their tasty goodness...
> rarely does this actually work.

fully popped --→ dud -→ reheated dud

washing out
zip locks
at your
own risk

Washing out resealable plastic bags previously
used to store meat or other greasy items with
the intention of reusing them: You end up
using too much water, and the bags still stink.

Using plastic bread bags for sandwich bags by cutting them into three pieces, folding over the ends to "lock in" freshness: Inevitably your daughter's sandwich will end up on the floor.

REFER TO **MULTITASKING BREAD BAGS** UNDER CHEAP STORIES, PAGE 194.

incisions

oops factor

Washing clothes labeled "dry clean only."
Your suits, shirts and skirts will be at least
one size smaller.

Underestimating how much plastic wrap is actually needed to cover a container: This chintzy act only results in overused plastic wrap to compensate for a weak seal.

structural
flaw

·ting·

Re-gifting, but forgetting who gave you the gift:
You might inadvertently give it back to them.

CHEAP
STORIES

PART OF THE ENJOYMENT OF WRITING THIS BOOK
HAS BEEN COLLECTING ANECDOTES FROM FRIENDS AND FAMILY.
BELIEVE IT OR NOT, THE FOLLOWING ARE TRUE STORIES.
(NAMES HAVE BEEN CHANGED TO PROTECT THE INNOCENT.)

SEW LOW

Greg discovered that his favorite dress shirt was missing a button and had a small hole in the armpit. An unskilled tailor, Greg opted to "donate" the distressed shirt to Goodwill charitable collections instead of repairing the garment with a needle and thread. The center accepted the gift, repaired the shirt, and placed it out on the sales rack. The following day, Greg went into the same Goodwill and bought his own shirt back for three dollars.

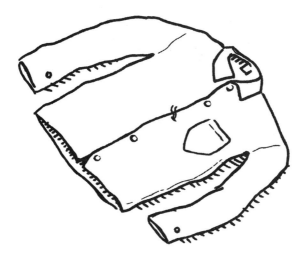

CHEAP LOVE

Sandy's parents have been married for fifty-five years. After thirty years, they got tired of purchasing Valentine's Day and anniversary cards for one another. Now they hit the card section together, find the perfect cards, then present them to each other right there in the store aisle. After reading them, they return the cards to their slots for sale. This way, they've shared the sentiment without the cost.

RECYCLING WATER

The outdoor plumbing had cracked, and Steve had no idea of how to fix it. Hiring a plumber seemed too expensive, so he simply shut off the water and used the dehumidifier water for his plants every morning.

SPEEDY STINKY SPORT

Mary's family decided to make a game out of the dying fluorescent bulb
in their bathroom. The challenge was to do their "business" and flush
before the light fully illuminated, even though they switched it on as
they entered. Any family member with enough talent to finish before the
light illuminated was admired. The game went on for three years before
a quick 15-minute repair provided the family with instant light when they
clicked the switch.

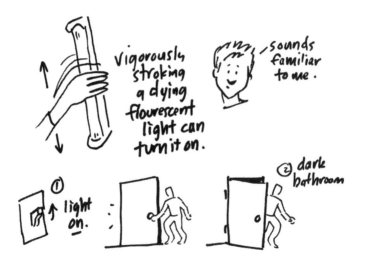

POPSICLE STICK HEALING

When Mac punched his arm through the upstairs window (he had his reasons), his mother chose to treat his bleeding elbow without consulting a doctor. By using a Telfa pad, gauze, athletic tape and two popsicle sticks, she made a straight-arm cast in about two minutes. He spent the next ten days with his arm extended. No stitches, no cast, no cost.

CEDAR SHAKIN'

Dan replaced his cedar shake roof a few years back. Level one cheapness: Rather than allowing the roofers to take the old shingles, he stacked them in the backyard to use as firewood. Level two cheapness: Dan sat in a lawn chair next to the old shingle pile and spent days methodically removing all the nails, saving them for reuse later. Level three cheapness: To this day, Dan searches the spot where the shingles were dumped, looking for more nails. He proudly boasts how many nails he's found since the pile disappeared.

GOLD-MEDAL CAR RIDES

After church, Roy's dad always stopped at the store to pick up a small bag of cashews (emphasis on small, because you know how expensive cashews are). He gave one cashew to each of the kids to keep in their mouth for the ten-mile trip home, testing to see if they could make the cashew last the entire ride. (Little did Roy know that this was actually a ploy to simply keep his travels quiet, not the Olympic competition he wanted so desperately to win.)

MULTITASKING BREAD BAGS

When Linda was growing up, her mom used to pack lunches for all seven kids. In order to save on purchasing sandwich bags, she would take a bread bag and cut it into three parts. If you got the bottom section it was a good day because your sandwich was secure. If you were unfortunate enough to get the middle or end pieces, your eagerness usually found the sandwich on the cafeteria floor. (See also Failed Attempts at Cheapness on page 182.)

THE TOWEL CYCLE OF LIFE

When Wanda and Bruce Smith got married, Wanda's mother-in-law passed along her bath towels because she wanted to buy new ones. The Smiths were cheap and poor back then, so they gladly accepted the gift and used them as their premier towels. Years went by, and soon they were ready to buy new towels themselves. Never ones to waste, they demoted the mother-in-law towels to tough, possibly permanently damaging roles such as cleaning doggie accidents and wiping up spilled paint. Once the towels began to wear out and tear, they were cut into rags. It's been twenty-two years since the Smiths received these treasures. May they rest in peace in the garbage soon.

EXTREMELY CHEAP SALT USAGE

An icy sidewalk may require salt, but Ann gingerly sprinkles the salt so as not to pour too much. She only uses salt on the driveway and walks where she thinks people may actually step. Then she takes it further. After the salt has finished melting the ice and is dried up, she sweeps it from the sidewalk and saves it to use again later. Wasted? No way!

BEWARE OF ENVELOPE REUSE

Erica dutifully uses return envelopes from unsolicited mail for charitable organizations or other such bills not paid by check. She just slaps a blank label on top of the address to make use of this otherwise wasted envelope. This practice backfired for her, however, and should be a lesson for us all. One day, she mailed her child support payment in one of these envelopes. Weeks later, she received a call regarding her failure to pay. She found out that the check had been cashed by a "hungry children" charitable organization. There must be some mistake! Yep, several, in fact: Have you ever noticed the bar code on the bottom of some return envelopes? As my friend discovered, the postal service reads the bar code (not the handwritten mailing address) to determine where an envelope is headed. Because Erica reused the "hungry children" group's return envelope, they received her check and managed to cash it despite being the incorrect payee.

THE GREEN SIDE OF CHEAP

BE CHEAP, BE GREEN. AS SILLY AS SOME OF THESE CHEAPISMS SEEM, BEING CHEAP CAN HELP SAVE THE ENVIRONMENT. THE FOLLOWING ARE JUST A FEW EXAMPLES.

1. In New York City alone, one less grocery bag per person each year would reduce waste by 5 million pounds and save $250,000 in disposal costs for the city. www.sierraclub.org

2. If everyone in the United States reused their tissue just once, it would save 4,301,999 boxes of tissues. *

3. About 53.3 percent of consumers planned to buy a costume for Halloween in 2005. If each person reused their costume instead of purchasing again the following year, that would save close to 150 million costumes! www.nrf.com

4. 135,582 pairs of underwear would be saved if each male in the United States wore a pair of underwear just one more time before he tossed it. *

5. Unsure where to toss your outdated toilet? Consider using crushed porcelain as yard décor. Reusing the material not only keeps discarded toilets out of landfills and closes the recycling loop, but it also reduces the need to mine gravel, thus saving money and benefiting the environment. www.papertrail.com

6. Electric dryers are among the top energy-consuming machines in a home, right behind refrigerators, lighting and water heaters. Because

the average dryer uses 875 kilowatt hours of electricity a year to dry clothing, it's a prime target for reducing global-warming pollution and saving money on your utility bill. Consider hanging clothes out to dry in the fresh summer air, or line drying clothing in your laundry room or basement. www.treehugger.com

7. If each person in Los Angeles took home their unused plastic utensils from a meal, 3,844,820 utensils would be conserved for future dinners. *

8. When you turn on an incandescent light bulb, only 10 percent of its electricity converts into visible light. The remaining 90 percent is wasted as heat. Using a 20-watt compact fluorescent bulb instead of a 75-watt incandescent bulb saves about 550kWh of electricity over its lifetime. If the electricity is produced from a coal-fired power plant, that savings represents about 500 pounds of coal. www.eia.doe.gov

9. Saving 400 toilet paper squares averages one regular-sized roll of toilet paper. *

10. 73,792 rolls of toilet paper would be saved each day in the entire state of Minnesota if all its residents reduced their toilet paper usage by two squares. *

11. A heavy coat of dust on a light bulb can block up to half of the light. www.worldwise.com

12. Plastic "cotton" swabs could take 50 to 100 years to decompose, whereas authentic cotton versions are gone in just 1 to 10 years. Plus, it's easier to break real cotton swabs in half! www.consrv.ca.gov

13. At about 35 percent, paper and paperboard products constitute the largest portion of municipal solid waste. www.epa.gov

14. 500 billion to 1 trillion plastic bags are used annually worldwide. In Taiwan an individual uses 900 bags per year. In Australia consumers use on average only 326 bags per year. United States retailers use 100 billion plastic bags, which cost them over $4 billion a year. www.onlinejournal.com *

15. If the average U.S. household were to reuse a paper plate at least once, the U.S. would use 628 million paper plates versus the whopping 125 billion it currently uses. *

16. Even after recycling, 11.8 percent of the 8 million tons of landfill is made up of plastic. www.howstuffworks.com

17. If individuals in the state of Texas used the cotton stuffers in vitamin or medicine bottles just once, it would save enough cotton to produce 583,000 pairs of jeans. www.cotton.org *

18. An average family of four spends approximately $29 a year on napkins. By taking home unused napkins from restaurants, the United States would save more than $15 million on paper napkins annually. *

19. Individuals in the United States spend approximately $326 a year on cosmetics. By extending the use of cosmetics twice as long as the suggested six months, the annual cost would drop to $19.9 billion each year. *

20. Using an electric oven costs 11.3 cents per hour versus the average furnace heating cost of 13.45 cents per hour. By leaving the oven door open after cooking, all households in Minnesota combined could save $40 million in heating costs. www.nppd.com *

21. On average, an office worker uses one sheet of paper every 12 minutes and one ream of paper every two-and-a-half weeks. *

22. After recycling, the total United States waste disposal is 49 million tons of paper, or 32.2 percent solid waste. www.howstuffworks.com

23. Appliance usage costs per month[+]:

Clock	16¢ / month
Curling iron	1.3¢ / hour
Garage-door opener	.10¢ / month
Satellite dish	$5.36 / month
Washing machine (cold/cold)	2.5¢ / load

Washing machine (warm/cold)	11.3¢ / load
Washing machine (hot/warm)	30.1¢ / load
Dryer (clothes)	41¢ / load
Microwave oven	12.6¢ / hour

24. Americans use five times more water than Europeans—100 to 125 gallons a day. Two-thirds of this consumption is in the bathroom. If Americans were to flush their toilets only half of the time, they would save 882 billion gallons of water a year. www.epa.gov *

25. 70 percent of Americans brush their teeth twice daily. On average, one tube of toothpaste costs $1 and lasts approximately one month. If an individual were to get an additional five uses out of the toothpaste tube, they could save up to $2 a year. In the state of California, that would be a savings of $72 million. www.epa.gov *

26. Of all the water on Earth, 97.5 percent is salt water and 2.5 percent is fresh water. A person can live about a month without food, but only about a week without water. The state of California uses almost 11 percent of all the fresh water in the United States. Texas, Idaho and Illinois combined use 28 percent. www.epa.gov *

* NOTE: THIS FACT IS BASED ON AUTHOR ESTIMATES USING ACTUAL POPULATIONS FROM WWW.CITYPOPULATION.DE.
+ THESE FIGURES ARE BASED ON AN ELECTRIC PRICE OF 8.14¢ PER KWH. WWW.NPPD.COM

CHEAPO
GLOSSARY

CHEAPO (ch p-o) n. A person who is most decidedly cheap.

> Consider yourself a Cheapo if you drive around town looking for the lowest gas prices.

CHEAPISM (ch p-izm) n. The act of saving money by the innovative use or non-use of materials and talents without regard to societal norms.

> Melding your slivers of soap together to make a larger bar is considered a good Cheapism.

CROFINGER (krō-fin-g r) n. The result of taking the well-intended, yet ill-advised suggestion of using only one square of toilet paper at a time (clearly considered a green cheap).

> "Aargh—I have Crofinger. Do you have any antibacterial soap?"

EXPIRATOR (eks'per-A-ter) n. A person who knowingly challenges the expiration dates on food, medication, etc.

> As an Expirator, my husband has been known to use medicine more than five years after the expiration date.

EXTRACTOTENACITY (ek-'strakt-oh-t 'nas- t-) n. The determination a Cheapo uses when trying to remove all the contents from peanut butter jars, sour cream containers, toothpaste tubes and soup cans.

Because I have so much Extractotenacity, I can get at least ten more uses out of a tube of toothpaste than the average person.

FREE RANGE FOOD (free rAnj food) n. Food that is consumed after extending the five second rule to ten seconds and longer, depending on the item.

She saw the candy-coated chocolate piece, otherwise know as Free Range Food, on the floor of her car and swiftly ate it.

HOPEINK (hope-inc) v. Displaying an inability to throw away an ill-performing pen or marker until it absolutely won't work again.

Even though the pen had failed her in the past, she was Hopeink it would work during the meeting.

KIDDERANG (kid-r-rang) n. A child who replaces grocery items when you come across a better deal on a similar item elsewhere in the store.

Her son, the Kidderang, was tired of running up and down the aisles to replace items.

LEFTOVER ROULETTE (left-Ov'r roo-let) n. When you go to the fridge and choose a leftover without any knowledge of the time of initial freshness. Passing the sight and smell test leaves only the taste test. (See page 115.)

After playing Leftover Roulette, Sam found himself battling stomach cramps.

MANTAPE (man-tAp) n. Duct tape—useful in so many ways.

"Honey, did you fix the molding that was falling off my car?" "I sure did. I used Mantape to keep it in place. It even matches your silver paint."

OPTIKEEPER (op-tee-keep-er) n. A person who saves all material, no matter how seemingly obsolete, on the slim chance that he may be able to use it for something later.

As an Optikeeper, he saves any excess parts when assembling manufactured items.

POOSMUDGE (poo-smudg) n. The tragedy that occurs when picking up dog doo with a reused bag that contains a hole.

Much to her dismay, she experienced Poosmudge halfway through her daily walk with Fido.

SUPERWEAR (süp-p r-wa( )r) n. Undergarments that can be worn despite stains, failing elastic and small holes.

Mother always warned me not to wear Superwear in case I ended up in an accident.

SWAMPSHOES (swämp shüz) n. Old, stinky tennis shoes worn in creeks and streams.

Warning! When not being worn, Swampshoes must stay in the garage.

SWOOP 'N' SCOOP (swüp N scüp) n. The act of quickly recovering spilled shower gel or shampoo from the floor during a shower.

Although she banged her head, her swift Swoop 'n' Scoop saved the precious gel from washing down the drain.

TIPDODGE (tip-dodg) v. Quickly grabbing your bags from bellboys in order to avoid having to tip.

By avoiding eye contact and taking immediate action he was able to Tipdodge.

TIPPYFILL (tip-E-fil) n. The act of balancing almost-empty bottles upside down to drain them into a fuller container.

She bumped the counter before the Tippyfill extraction was complete.

WIRE-THINGY (wir thing-e) n. An invention made from a coat hanger primarily used to thread belts and unclog drains. (Refer to The Tool under Cheapo Inventions, page 172.)

"Hon, can you grab the Wire-Thingy? The kitchen drain is clogged again."

SCORE YOUR CHEAPNESS

Now, add up all of the points you've earned while reading this book and discovering your cheapisms. Use the next page to tally your score and make important notations. Match your score to the values below to find out just how cheap you really are.

SCORING:

0–125 points: You have wasted your time reading this book unless you can actually learn something from it. You obviously are a big-time free spender and do not adhere to the principles held sacred by true Cheapos. Don't be discouraged; progress is possible.

126–250 points: You have some traits of the truly cheap, but you seem to lack the resolve to make it a guiding factor in your everyday life. Take baby steps and embrace one new cheapism each day. You have potential.

251–375 points: You're our kind of person: frugal, yet sensible, cheap and proud of your standing.

376–500 points: There are issues in your past that have led you to this rank. Since you have come this far, pushing you over the edge won't take much.

Over 500 points: Set this book down now and submit your name and story for consideration in the Cheapo Hall of Fame at www.thecheapbook. com. You are a true inspiration to Cheapos around the world, and your cheapness should be worn like a badge of honor.

SCORING PAGE

Tally your points here

CHAPTER	SCORE	CHAPTER	SCORE	CHAPTER	SCORE
1		6		11	
2		7		12	
3		8		13	
4		9		14	
5		10		15	
SUBTOTAL		SUBTOTAL		SUBTOTAL	
TOTAL					

INDEX

THE END

Add to our growing list of Cheapo behaviors, inventions, failures and more.
Visit our web site at www.thecheapbook.com and you might find your
Cheapism published in our next book!